Contents

INTRODUCTION

The Gardens of Eden is either a happy coincidence or a sign of the times. Published in early April, the book goes into the homes of gardeners who are fashioning their environments into lush green landscapes. The book highlights the innovative ways urbanites are building oases amid concrete jungles, the creative liberties modern gardeners are taking with residential spaces and the sustainable benefits of having a garden. And it seems that the world is ready to reinvigorate their green thumb has seen a surge in searches for "backyard gardening." Getting into gardening, however, can seem like a daunting task as a life is literally in your hands.

If a fruit and vegetable garden is on your wish-list, but you just don't have room outside, then consider mixing these alongside your ornamental plants. Most fruits and veggies will grow perfectly fine amongst the different perennials and annual flowers. As an example, you could plant a row of lettuce to line the edging of a particular flower bed. Now, it is possible to include a variety of edible fruits and vegetables during your backyard gardening.

Good soil is key to healthy plants. Soft, black soil is often desirable. Soil with lots of clay will need more work and can be helped by adding compost. Some plants like soil that has been turned either by hand or rototiller. Other plants grow better with little disturbance to their environment. It's important to do basic research on what you're planting. Adding compost is often a good idea because it provides extra nutrients. Don't be afraid of earthworms since they are a sign of healthy soil and will maintain your good soil.

CHAPTER ONE

Gardening, the laying out and care of a plot of ground devoted partially or wholly to the growing of plants such as flowers, herbs, or vegetables.

Gardening can be considered both as an art, concerned with arranging plants harmoniously in their surroundings, and as a science, encompassing the principles and techniques of plant cultivation. Because plants are often grown in conditions markedly different from those of their natural environment, it is necessary to apply to their cultivation techniques derived from plant physiology, chemistry, and botany, modified by the experience of the planter. The basic principles involved in growing plants are the same in all parts of the world, but the practice naturally needs much adaptation to local conditions.

For the main history of garden development, see the article garden and landscape design: Historical development.

The Nature Of Gardening

Gardening in its ornamental sense needs a certain level of civilization before it can flourish. Wherever that level has been attained, in all parts of the world and at all periods, people have made efforts to shape their environment into an attractive display. The instinct and even enthusiasm for gardening thus appear to arise from some primitive response to nature, engendering a wish to produce growth and harmony in a creative partnership with it.

It is possible to be merely an admiring spectator of gardens. However, most people who cultivate a domestic plot also derive satisfaction from involvement in the processes of tending plants. They find that the necessary attention to the seasonal changes, and to the myriad small "events" in any shrubbery or herbaceous border, improves their understanding and appreciation of gardens in general.

A phenomenal upsurge of interest in gardening began in Western countries after World War II. A lawn with flower beds and perhaps a vegetable patch has become a sought-after advantage to home ownership. The increased interest produced an unprecedented expansion of business among horticultural suppliers, nurseries, garden centres, and seedsmen. Books, journals, and newspaper columns on garden practice have found an eager readership, while television and radio programs on the subject have achieved a dedicated following.

Several reasons for this expansion suggest themselves. Increased leisurein the industrial nations gives more people the opportunity to enjoy this relaxing pursuit. The increased public appetite for self-sufficiency in basic skills also encourages people to take up the spade. In the kitchen, the homegrown potato or ear of sweet corn rewards the gardener with a sense of achievement, as well as with flavour superior to that of store-bought produce. An increased awareness of threats to the natural environment and the drabness of many inner cities stir some people to cultivate the greenery and colour around their own doorsteps. The bustle of 20th-century life leads more individuals to rediscover the age-old tranquillity of gardens.

The varied appeal of gardening

The attractions of gardening are many and various and, to a degree perhaps unique among the arts and crafts, may be experienced by any age group and at all levels of ambition. At its most elemental, but not least valuable, the gardening experience begins with the child's wonder that a packet of seeds will produce a charming festival of colour. At the adult level, it can be as simple as helping to raise a good and edible carrot, and it can give rise to almost parental pride. At higher levels of appreciation, it involves an understanding of the complexity of the gardening process, equivalent to a chess game with nature, because the variables are so many.

The gardening experience may involve visiting some of the world's great gardens at different seasons to see the relation of individual groups of plants, trees, and shrubs to the whole design; to study the positioning of plants in terms of their colour, texture, and weight of leaf or blossom; and to appreciate the use of special features such as ponds or watercourses, pavilions, or rockeries. Garden visiting on an international scale provides an opportunity to understand the broad cultural influences, as well as the variations in climate and soil, that have resulted in so many different approaches to garden making.

The appeal of gardening is thus multifaceted and wide in range. The garden is often the only place where someone without special training can exercise creative impulses as designer, artist, technician, and scientific observer. In addition, many find it a relaxing and therapeutic pursuit. It is not surprising that the garden, accorded respect as a part of nature and a place of contemplation, holds a special place in the spiritual life of many.

Practical and spiritual aspects of gardening are shown in an impressive body of literature. In Western countries manuals of instruction date to classical Greece and Rome. Images of plants and gardens are profuse in the works of the major poets, from Virgil to Shakespeare, and on to some of the moderns.

Another of gardening's attractions is that up to a certain level it is a simple craft to learn. The beginner can produce pleasing results without the exacting studies and practice required by, for example, painting or music. Gardens are also forgiving to the inexperienced to a certain degree. Nature's exuberance will cover up minor errors or short periods of neglect, so gardening is an art practiced in a relatively nonjudgmental atmosphere. While tolerant in many respects, nature does, however, present firm reminders that all gardening takes place within a framework of natural law; and one important aspect of the study of the craft is to learn which of these primal rules are imperatives and which may be stretched.

Control and cooperation

Large areas of gardening development and mastery have concentrated on persuading plants to achieve what they would not have done if left in the wild and therefore "natural" state. Gardens at all times have been created through a good deal of control and what might be called interference. The gardener attends to a number of basic processes: combating weeds and pests; using space to allay the competition between plants; attending to feeding, watering, and pruning; and conditioning the soil. Above this fundamental level, the gardener assesses and accommodates the unique complex of temperature, wind, rainfall, sunlight, and shade found within his own garden boundaries. A major part of the fascination of gardening is that in problems and potential no one garden is quite like another; and it is in finding the most imaginative solutions to challenges that the gardener demonstrates artistry and finds the subtler levels of satisfaction.

Different aesthetics require different balances between controlling nature and cooperating with its requirements. The degree of control depends on the gardener's objective, the theme and identity he is aiming to create. For example, the English wild woodland style of gardening in the mid-19th century dispensed with controls after planting, and any interference, such as pruning, would have been misplaced. At the other extreme is the Japanese dry-landscape garden, beautifully composed of rock and raked pebbles. The artistic control in this type of garden is so firm and refined that the intrusion of a single "natural" weed would spoil the effect.

Choice of plants

The need for cooperation with nature is probably most felt by the amateur gardener in choosing the plants he wants to grow. The range of plants available to the modern gardener is remarkably rich, and new varieties are constantly being offered by nurseries. Most of the shrubs and flowers used in the Western world are descendants of plants imported from other countries. Because they are nonnative, they present the gardener with some of his most interesting problems but also with the possibility of an enhanced display. Plants that originated in subtropical regions, for example, are naturally more sensitive to frost. Some, like rhododendrons or azaleas, originated in an acid soil, mainly composed of leaf mold. Consequently, they will not thrive in a chalky or an alkaline soil. Plant breeding continues to improve the adaptability of such exotic plants, but the more closely the new habitat resembles the original, the better the plant will flourish. Manuals offer solutions to most such problems, and the true gardener will always enjoy finding his own. In such experiments, he may best experience his work as part of the historical tradition of gardening.

Historical Background

Early history

Western gardening had its origins in Egypt some 4,000 years ago. As the style spread, it was changed and adapted to different localities and climates, but its essentials remained those of disciplined lines and groupings of plants, usually in walled enclosures. Gardening was introduced into Europe through the expansion of Roman rule and, second, by way of the spread of Islam into Spain. Though clear evidence is lacking, it is presumed that Roman villas outside the confines of Italy contained native and imported plants, hedges, fruit trees, and vines, in addition to herbs for medicinal and culinary purposes.

In medieval times the monasteries were the main repositories of gardening knowledge and the important herbal lore. Though little is certainly known about the design and content of the monastic garden, it probably consisted of a walled courtyard built around a well or an arbour, with colour provided by flowers (some of which, including roses and lilies, served as ecclesiastical symbols), all of which maintained the ancient idea of the garden as a place of contemplation.

The earliest account of gardening in English, The Feate of Gardening, dating from about 1400, mentions the use of more than 100 plants, with instructions on sowing, planting, and grafting of trees and advice on cultivation of herbs such as parsley, sage, fennel, thyme, camomile, and saffron. The vegetables mentioned include turnip, spinach, leek, lettuce, and garlic.

Early gardening was largely for utility. The emergence of the garden as a form of creative display properly began in the 16th century. The Renaissance, with its increased prosperity, brought an upsurge of curiosity about the natural world and, incidentally, stirred interest in composing harmonious forms in the garden.

This awakening took especially firm root in Elizabethan England, which notably developed the idea that gardens were for enjoyment and delight. Echoing the Renaissance outlook, the mood of the period was one of exuberance in gardening, seen in the somewhat playful arrangements of Tudor times, with mazes, painted statuary, and knot gardens (consisting of beds in which various types of plants were separated by dwarf hedges). Flowers began to appear profusely in paintings and, as mentioned above, were used by poets in their verbal images.

This enthusiasm was accompanied by an earnest search for knowledge, and the period saw the birth of botanical science. A leading figure in this work was Carolus Clusius (Charles de l'Écluse), whose botanical skills and introduction of the tulip and other bulbous plants to the botanical gardens at Leiden, Netherlands, laid the foundation for Dutch prominence in international horticulture. The earliest botanical gardenwas that of Pisa (1543), followed by that of Padua (1545). The first in England was founded at Oxford in 1621, followed by Scotland's first, at Edinburgh, in 1667. The gardens at Kew, near London, were founded almost a century later, in 1759. These centres of experiment and learning have contributed greatly to the art and science of horticulture.

The advances from the simple medieval style were marked and rapid at this time. The English statesman and scholar Francis Bacon could already, by 1625, advance a sophisticated and almost modern conceptionof the garden in his essay "On Gardens." He saw it as a place that should be planted for year-round enjoyment, offering a wide range of experiences through colour, form and scent, exercise and repose. The flower garden, already well established by the early 17th century, was set against a background of tall, clipped hedges and neatly scythed lawns. The taste of the time, as contemporary lists show, was for perfumed varieties such as carnations, lavender, sweet marjoram, musk roses, and poppies.

The plant trade

As interest in gardening developed in Europe, the new trade of nurseryman was established, and the trade became highly important to the spread of knowledge and materials. By the end of the 17th century, nurserymen were relatively numerous in England, France, and the Low Countries, with keen customers among the nobility and gentry for all the exotica they could provide. The catalog of the Tradescant family's private botanical garden in London listed 1,600 plants in 1656. A number of them had been brought back by the family from visits to Virginia. These early exotica from the New World included now familiar plants such as the Michaelmas daisy, the Virginia creeper, hamamelis, goldenrod, the first perennial lupine, and such fine autumn-colouring trees as liquidambar and the staghorn sumac. The work of the nurserymen thus spread new plants more widely and, as breeding skills developed, contributed to the acclimatizing of foreign imports.

Vegetables and fruits

The history of vegetables is imprecise. Though familiar types, including the radish, turnip, and onion, are known to have been in cultivation from early times, it is fairly supposed that they were meagre and would bear little clear resemblance to modern equivalents. The early range available to European gardens and, later, to those in America, included such native plants as kale, parsnips, and the Brussels sprout family, with peas and broad beans grown as field crops.

The Romans introduced the globe artichoke, leek, cucumber, cabbage, asparagus, and the Mediterranean strain of garlic to their imperial territory wherever these plants would flourish. Among plants imported to Europe from the Americas were the scarlet runner bean and tomato (both originally grown for ornament), corn (maize), and the vastly important potato. The numerous herbs in use were mostly native to European locations. One curiosity to the modern mind is that certain flowers, such as marigolds, violets, and primroses, were used as flavourings in the kitchen.

The cultivation of fruit trees was one of the most advanced skills and interests from the 16th century onward. Pride was taken in variety, and, judging by the opulent still-life paintings of the period, the quality was remarkably high. Among the challenges bravely taken up in the 17th century in northern Europe was the growing of orange and lemon trees, though this was done more for the pleasure of their evergreen qualities than for their fruit. The catalog of the British royal gardens in 1708 shows 14 varieties of cherry, 14 apricots, 58 kinds of peach and nectarine, 33 plums, eight figs, 23 vines, 29 pears, and numerous varieties of apple.

The French style

The most favoured style for great house gardens in Europe during much of this period derived from the influence of the French designer André Le Nôtre, creator of the gardens at Versailles. The French style represented an extreme of formality, with box-edged parterres (elaborate and geometrical beds) typically placed near the residence to provide an arranged view. Trees were grouped in neat plantations or in bold lines along avenues, with terraces and statuary carefully placed to emphasize the architectural symmetry of the grand manner. The widespread adoption of this style among the European nobility and gentry reflected the potency of French cultural influence at the time. It was also related, on a practical basis, to the limited availability of planting materials, especially those offering autumn and winter display.

The change to a more natural style of gardening came about when, in the latter part of the 18th century, the opinion arose among leading gardeners, particularly those of the English gentry, that the formal manner brought with it a certain monotony. The increasing importation of foreign plants also brought with it opportunities for a large-scale transformation.

The plant hunters

The early importation of plants to Europe was managed through informal channels, following the increase in exploration and the spread of empires. Seeds and tubers were sent home by diplomats and missionaries, sea captains and travelers. An example of this type of collecting is afforded by Henry Compton, bishop of London, whose diocese included the American colonies. He was an avid collector, and he corresponded with like-minded experts in Europe and America and thus brought numerous fine plants to his exceptional garden in Fulham, west London. He also encouraged his missionaries to send home seeds. From one such source in Virginia came the Magnolia virginiana, the first magnolia to be cultivated. This was the beginning of what became known as the American garden, based upon magnolias, azaleas, and other woodland species.

As the appetite for exotica developed, plant collecting around the world became more systematized. Expeditions to foreign parts were organized and financed by nurserymen, botanical gardens, or syndicates of private gardeners. The botanist plant hunters thus sent out were exceptional and patient. They were required to endure long voyages and residence for up to several years in an often hostile environment. Their goal was to find the plant in flower, return in due season to collect seed, then see their delicate specimens back to Europe through varying climatic zones.

North America's potential to yield countless new specimens was recognized early: the first book on American plants, published in London in 1577, was entitled Joyfull Newes out of the New Founde Worlde and was in itself a hint of the excited spirit of contemporary gardening. The jacaranda, flowering catalpa, and wisteria were among the finds made by Compton's missionaries in the Carolinas. An early resident collector in North America was John Bartram, regarded as the founder of American botany. He settled on a farm near Philadelphia in 1728 and, in 30 years of collecting in the Alleghenies, Carolinas, and other areas of North America, sent some 200 important plants to British gardens in sufficient quantity that they became widespread there.

The extremely rich west coast of North America was not exploited by plant collectors until the early 19th century. The contemporary importance of such discoveries is suggested by the fact that, in their celebrated crossing of the American continent in 1804–06, Lewis and Clark found time to collect the seeds of Mahonia aquifolium and Symphoricarpos racemosus. Perhaps the most distinguished collector among an exceptional fraternity was David Douglas, one of the numerous Scotsmen who contributed to international botany. His expeditions to the North American Far West brought to Europe such important timber trees as the Douglas fir, the Sitka spruce, the Monterey pine, and a number of now familiar shrubs such as Garrya elliptica and Ribes sanguineum. The California annuals he discovered made a lasting impact on the colour of Western gardens. In the 19th century, plant collectors began to explore South America, where two Cornish brothers, William and Thomas Lobb, gained prominence. They are credited with carrying back to Europe the monkey puzzle tree (Araucaria araucana), native to the Andes mountains; the Berberis darwinii; and the Escallonia macrantha.

Branch of the monkey puzzle tree (Araucaria araucana), an evergreen ornamental and timber conifer native to the Andes mountains of South America.

Collectors went to a number of countries in the 19th century, but the most important area was China. Its flora was more intact than that in the West, because the erosions of the Ice Age had been less severe for climatic reasons, and it had a long history of skilled gardening. Plant collection was difficult, however, because for many years the only foreigners allowed to travel within its borders were Jesuit priests. They aided botanists by sending many specimens to Paris and London. The first professional collector to live in China was William Kerr, who sent out 238 new plants. Real exploration of the interior did not begin until the 1840s. China, Japan, and the Himalayas produced unparalleled riches in rhododendrons, azaleas, flowering cherries, ornamental maples, roses, lilies, primulas, poppies, kerrias, and quinces.

The conditions for transporting plants from such distances had been much improved by Nathaniel B. Ward's invention of the wardian case, an airtight glass box that protected the plants from sea air and harsh climate. Gradually almost all regions and countries were visited, and new plants and their progeny were dispersed around the Western world. And still the search for new specimens continues.

From the 19th century

By the early 19th century, with the expansion of the horticultural trade, gardening had become international in scope. Numerous handbooks spread knowledge. The founding of new garden and botanical societies, such as the London (later Royal) Horticultural Society, helped to increase interest, encourage science, and raise standards. Such moves signaled the rise of the small leisure gardener; a floral retreat was no longer the sole property of the rich. It now extended from the manor to the small suburban garden.

Gardens in North America had generally been smaller and trimmer than their European counterparts, with box edgings and pleached trees (that is, lines of trees allowed to grow with branches interlaced to form a screen), as seen in the reconstructed gardens of Williamsburg, Virginia. The "natural" gardening style (known on the European continent as the English style), which had overtaken earlier formality, allowed wider use of plant varieties. This approach became the pervasive trend in the west, notably through the views of John Claudius Loudon, whose Encyclopaedia of Gardening (1822) set the pattern of domestic cultivation over a long period with a style known as Gardenesque. His style encouraged the individual qualities of garden elements while ensuring that together they made a harmonious blend.

The natural style was further enhanced by an English artist and landscape architect, Gertrude Jekyll. In her opinion, the first purpose of a garden is to give happiness and repose of mind. With experience derived from the richly floral cottage gardens of Surrey, she developed the idea of supporting plants with an architectural base and allowing them to grow in a free form, encouraging natural shape and creating harmonious relationships of colour.

The period saw much progress in garden equipment and supplies. Heated greenhouses had been in use since the late 17th century, and mass production led to great strides in nursery gardening. The modern, bladed lawn mower was first seen in a design of 1832; in more recent times the application of the jet-engine principle led to the hover mower. Fertilizer development was also important, from the discovery of superphosphate to the devising of modern kinds of foliar feeding.

In the second half of the 20th century, interest in gardening brought in new adherents in unprecedented numbers; they were advised and encouraged by numerous publications and by television and radio programs. Though the process was very gradual, domestic gardening became somewhat more adventurous. Among the more ambitious, designs took a multiplicity of forms, from the Japanese garden, producing an austere magic out of rock and pebble, to the other extreme of the wild country garden, virtually left to seed itself. Increasing numbers of professional designers at their best set high standards to emulate. But the art of gardening still depends on a simple empathy with the needs and nature of living things. Symbolic of this essential, the spade has remained much the same implement that it had been in medieval times.

How to Start a New Garden

You may have visions of drifts of color, wildflower prairies, or bushels of tomatoes, but get your feet wet first with some gardening basics. For flower gardens, choose a site close to the door or with a good view from a favorite window. Place your garden where you'll see and enjoy it often. This will also motivate you to garden more.

The front lawn shown here is small, but the homeowners still found an attractive, sunny spot to add some color and curb appeal. No matter how busy they are, they can enjoy their garden every time they pull into their driveway or look out their front window.

Evaluate and Choose a Site

If you have your heart set on growing a specific plant, check to see what growing conditions it requires. Vegetables will need at least six hours of sun exposure a day. The same goes for most flowering plants. However, there are still many to choose from for a partially shaded site. If you want to start a garden where there is mostly shade, your choices are going to be more limited but not prohibitive.

The folks in this picture have a partially shaded front entrance. They could easily add a small garden along the walkway where they could enjoy it, making their entrance more of a focal point.

Also, take into consideration when the sun hits your site. The afternoon sun will be hotter and more drying than the morning sun. Many plants turn their faces toward the sun, so if your view of the garden is from a west window, your flowers may face away from you in the afternoon. Evaluate other elements of exposure such as high, drying winds or heavy foot traffic.

Once you know where you'd like to try your first garden, you must use a hose or extension cord to try laying it out on the ground. Figure out the space it will take up.

Examine the Soil

Once you know where you want to plant, it's time to check the soil. Soil testing is the least glamorous part of gardening, but the most important. At the very least, check your soil's pH. This will tell you how acid or alkaline your soil is. Plants cannot take up nutrients unless the soil's pH is within an acceptable range. Most plants like a somewhat neutral pH, 6.2 to 6.8, but some are even more particular than that. If you are growing plants from the nursery, check the plant tag for specifics. If no pH preference is listed, a neutral range is fine.

You may also want to check the texture of your soil or even the nutrients and minerals in it. You can have that done at your local Cooperative Extension office and some nurseries. Soil texture refers to whether it is sandy, heavy clay, rocky, or the ideal sandy loam. Whatever the texture, it can be improved with the addition of organic matter such as compost.

Prepare the Bed

This is no one's favorite garden chore, but there's no way around it. Your chosen site will probably have grass on it or at least weeds. These must be cleared somehow before you can plant anything. Tilling without removing the grass or weeds is best done in the fall so that the grass will have a chance to begin decomposing during the winter. Even so, you will probably see new grass and weeds emerging in the spring. It's better to either remove the existing vegetation completely or to smother it.

A sharp flat-edged spade can be used to slice out the sod. If you have poor soil and need to amend it with organic matter or other nutrients, removing the sod may be your best bet so that you can till in the amendments.

Removing sod can be heavy work, and you wind up losing good topsoil along with the sod. If your soil is in relatively good shape, it is possible to leave the grass in place and build on top of it. Place a thick layer (eight to 10 sheets) of newspaper over the garden bed and wet it thoroughly. Then cover the newspaper with 4 to 6 inches of good soil. The newspaper will eventually decompose, and the turf and weeds will be smothered. There may be some defiant weeds that poke through, but not so many you can hand weed them. Starting with good soil means you won't have to add a lot of artificial fertilizer to your garden. If you've fed the soil with amendments, the soil will feed your plants.

Choosing What You'd Like to Grow

This is harder than you might think. If you are starting small, you have to limit yourself to a handful of plants. If you are growing vegetables, you must start with what you like to eat and what you can't find fresh locally. Corn takes a lot of space and remains in the garden a long time before it's ready to be eaten. If you have corn farms nearby, you might want to use your small garden for vegetables that give a longer harvest such as tomatoes, lettuce, and beans.

Flower gardens can be even harder. Start with what colors you like. Rather than basing your dream on a photograph from a magazine, take a look at what your neighbors are growing successfully. They may even be able to give you a division or two.

Take a walk around a couple of garden centers and read the plant labels. Then play with combining the plants that strike your eye until you find a combination of three to five plants that please you. Make sure all the plants have the same growing requirements (sun, water, pH, etc.) and that none of them are going to require more care than you can give them.

Keep the variety of plants limited. It makes a better composition to have more plants of fewer varieties than to have one of this and one of that.

Planting

Sometimes you have to plant when you have the time, even if that's high noon on a Saturday. But the ideal time to plant is on a still, overcast day. The point is, stress your new plants as little as possible.

• Water the plants in their pots the day before you intend to plant.

• Don't remove all the plants from their pots and leave them sitting in the sun for the roots to dry out.

• If the roots are densely packed or growing in a circle, tease them apart so they will stretch out and grow into the surrounding soil.

• Bury the plant to the depth it was in the pot. Too deep and the stem will rot. Too high and the roots will dry out.

• Don't press down hard on the plants as you cover them. Watering will settle them into the ground.

• Water your newly planted garden as soon as it is planted and make sure it gets at least 1 inch of water per week. You may have to water more often in hot, dry summers. Let your plants tell you how much water they need. Some wilting in noonday sun is normal. Wilting in the evening is stress.

Mulch

You hear a lot about mulching lately, but it does make a major difference in a garden. Mulch conserves water, blocks weeds, and cools the soil. Organic mulches such as shredded or chipped bark, compost, straw, and shredded leaves will also improve the soil's quality.

Plastic mulches are nice in a vegetable garden to heat the soil around warm-season crops such as tomatoes, peppers, melons, and squash.

Whatever mulch you choose, apply it soon after planting, before new weeds sprout. Apply a 2- to 4-inch-thick layer of mulch, avoiding direct contact with the plant stems. Piling mulch around the stem can lead to rotting and can provide cover for munching mice and voles.

Label Your Plants and Keep Garden Records

Keep a record of what you have planted or, better yet, keep the labels that came with your plants. This will help answer any questions about what the plant may need if it starts looking poorly and will remind you next year of what you liked and what didn't work. It also helps to take pictures and label them. You'll remember color combinations and favorite plants.

If you start a garden journal, you can also record how plants perform, when flowers are in bloom, how large the harvest was, and all kinds of information that will help you make a better garden next year.

Common Gardening Mistakes

Gardeners seem to prefer learning the hard way. In spite of all the gardening books we browse through, and the classes we attend, mistakes are invariably made.

Here's a sample of the ones many have made and regretted.

Not Preparing the Beds

Most of us have made this mistake, some out of ignorance, and others due to sheer laziness.

When the little seeds and seedling go into the damp earth in spring, it seems the tiny planting holes we make with our fingers or a small hand shovel are room enough for them.

But the soil soon dries out and becomes rock hard. If the roots of the young plants cannot penetrate into the soil, you'll end up with stunted plants.

Digging and double digging the garden beds and adding in plenty of compost and leaf mold makes the soil loose enough for good root run. And this backbreaking work has to be done before you plant things.

Making raised beds is another option if you don't want to dig deep.

Leaving Out Soil Amendment

We tend to forget that soil is like a living organism, always changing and evolving.

Soil conditions can fluctuate with the amount of rainfall, soil runoff and lack of drainage. Some plants deplete certain soil nutrients more than the others.

Heavy rains can leach away the limestone you recently added to raise the pH of your broccoli bed.

It pays to check the soil for pH level and mineral profile every growing season and make necessary amendments a few weeks before planting time.

Then test again to make sure things are perfect for the plants that are getting ready to go in.

Organic matter has a modulating effect on soil chemistry, so the more humus your soil has, the lesser the chemical fluctuations.

Add plenty of compost and cured manure to your vegetable beds.

Good soil is particularly important for your veggies garden since you need healthy plants that produce high-quality food.

Overwatering

Overwatering is like killing with too much love. Most over enthusiastic gardeners are guilty of this crime.

Frequent watering may be necessary until seedlings and cuttings get established. But once they have developed a good root system, water them at regular intervals.

The roots of most plants hate sitting in water. Like every other plant tissue, roots need to breathe.

They literally drown if all the air pockets in the soil are filled with water all the time. Even when the top soil looks dry, the lower layers could be soaking wet.

Frequently watered plants remain tender, and wilt very easily in the sun.

When the interval between subsequent watering is gradually increased, plants toughen up and learn to be survivors.

However, too much water stress can decrease the yield of some vegetables.

Shallow Watering

This is another watering mistake committed by those who water their plants with a handheld garden hose.

You spray the top growth, washing down the dust on the leaves and giving the entire plant a nice shower.

Satisfied, you move on unmindful of the fact that the roots have got very little water. When you see the plants looking rather tired in the afternoon sun, you may give them another quick shower.

Plants drink water through their roots.

Wilted crowns do recover rapidly when they are sprayed with water, but that is because it helps cut down the transpiration rate.

Shallow watering results in shallow root run. Plants become dependent on frequent watering.

They become prone to toppling over and wilting quickly since their roots have not grown deep into the soil to anchor them and to draw water from the reservoirs in the lower layers of soil.

Cut on the frequency of watering, but water the plants deeply every time.

Drip irrigation or a leaky hose watering system ensures deep watering.

They help save water too.

Planting Sun Lovers in the Shade

We all know plants have this unique ability to make food in their leaves with just sunlight, water and air. But sometimes we plant a tomato variety guaranteed to be a prolific bearer close to a tree.

We may be overjoyed at the luxurious growth, only to be disappointed by the low yield. The poor plant was making a lot of leaves to maximize food production, but it just wasn't enough.

There are some woodland plants that have evolved to survive in shady spots, but if you plant sun-loving plants there, they just will not thrive.

Tomatoes and most other veggies do best in areas where they can get uninterrupted sun throughout the day.

If you mainly have a shady garden, you cannot hope to grow a lot of vegetables other than some greens. Clear out an area for your vegetable patch.

Planting Out of Season

It is hard to believe seasons have such a hold on plants.

Many of us probably have planted seeds or cuttings at the wrong time of the year and watch them put out a bit of growth in the beginning and then quit.

Seasons are not much of an issue in tropical areas as long as the young plants are given plenty of water.

But it is quite another story up north.

Planting out tender seedling too early in spring leaves them at the mercy of late frosts. Delay a bit, and you may miss the chance to get vigorous growth and yield before the rising temperatures play spoilsport.

Cool season veggies and summer flowers have to be planted at their respective times.

Beware of end-of-season bargain offers by mail-order companies. By the time the order reaches you, it might be too late to plant them.

Some seeds are viable for only a short period, so preserving them for the next season may not be a good idea.

Follow the gardening calendar of your area and listen to the advice of local gardeners for best results.

Not Pruning Bushes and Trees

Pruning is hard work, but going lax on this seasonal task is one mistake new gardeners make.

With bushes grown for ornamental purposes, the prized shape and structure are soon lost.

The yield of fruit trees and berry bushes practically depends on meticulous pruning.

Left unpruned, the unnecessary branches and suckers zap them of all the energy that should have been directed towards flowering and fruit setting.

Some fruits grow only on new growth, so unless you prompt the plant to put out new shoots by hard pruning every year, you will be left without much fruit in the next season.

When you plant an ornamental/fruit tree or shrub, take pains to learn the right pruning technique.

It is even more important than watering and fertilizing schedules.

Hard Pruning at the Wrong Time

Have you ever pruned a hydrangea bush real hard in fall because it looked nearly dead?

You have probably removed all the dormant flower buds that would have bloomed the following year. Some plants bear flowers on old branches while others put out new flowering branches after pruning.

You should first learn about the flowering pattern of your bush and schedule the pruning accordingly.

Since pruning instigates new growth in most plants, those that bear flowers and fruits late in the growing season should be pruned once they have gone into dormancy.

Early pruning will make them put out tender shoots that will suffer frost damage.

Spring flowering trees and bushes can be pruned immediately after they have finished the show so that they get a long window to develop new growth before the growing season is over.

Maintain a pruning calendar for the plants in your garden to avoid mistakes.

Using Weed Killers on the Wrong day

You sprayed the herbicide on a patch of lawn overgrown with weeds, but the next day you find the nearby flower beds decimated.

There are selective herbicides that kill only the dicot weeds in the lawn and spare the grass. But the spray was carried by the wind to the dicots growing happily in the flower beds too.

Another mistake is using these chemicals when there's any danger of rains.

The runoff water will carry them off to wreak damage elsewhere. Chemical herbicides are best avoided, but if you do use them in your garden, choose sunny and windless days.

More importantly, some garden weeds posses extraordinary health benefits.

Make sure you know what they are and don't kill these off!

Planting Invasive Plants

Almost every gardener has fallen in love with a beautiful plant on his/her travels and has brought it home, not realizing they are considered noxious weeds in that area.

Just because you don't see certain plants in your locality, it doesn't mean they are not invasive.

Probably years of eradication measures and campaigning or strict rules have managed to keep them out, and you could have just undone all that.

Whether you gather seeds or plants from the wild or get planting materials from a distant friend or relative, or order them online, check beforehand if they are invasive in your area or not.

Once established, it is hard work, or nearly impossible, to root them out.

Planting Single Self-Sterile Plants

Have you purchased a berry bush or a young tree and waited for years only to be disappointed when none of the flowers turned into fruit?

If you have planted a self-sterile variety, you have two options: get rid of it or plant another one and wait for years again.

Some blueberry plants need two of the same type for successful pollination.

But it takes two different types of apple trees to give you fruit. Not only that, they should have the same blooming time.

Some apple trees produce sterile pollen, so you will need a third tree in the premises. It is a complex matter.

Some plums and pears are only partially self-sterile, and they manage to grow a few fruit. But they do much better in company.

If you don't want to try your luck, choose your plants with the help of knowledgeable suppliers, or stick to self-fertile varieties.

Scaring Away Pollinators with Pesticides

Being too handy with pesticides is a big mistake overzealous gardener make.

We are not talking about contaminating the earth here, although it is a great concern.

If you find too few vegetables and fruits after meticulously watering and fertilizing your plants and keeping off pests and weeds with frequent spraying, you could have scared off the pollinators.

It is hard to watch pests chomping away on your well-tended veggies, but remember that all the critters visiting your vegetable patch are not your enemies.

You need insect pollinators to ensure a good crop.

Planting Trees too Close to the House

You had zeroed in on the perfect tree for your landscape after extensive research, but now you are contemplating cutting it down.

You had made the mistake of planting it too close to the house.

The fully grown tree is literally a threat to your safety, let alone other problems like too much shade, constant dampness and fallen leaves and flowers making a mess around the house.

It is never a good idea to plant tall trees close to your home. You may think you can keep it under control with regular pruning, but who will control the roots beneath the soil?

They can spread and swell, making the foundation of the house unstable.

CHAPTER TWO
Importance of Backyard Gardens

Backyard gardens are relatively small areas around homes we use to grow food for ourselves and the family. The practice has been going on for ages but this practice is declining in our region for obvious reasons. We often presume food can always be obtained from the open market, so why waste time grow our own in a garden? or "… don't have the time to work on a garden", and a number of other reasons.

However, we strongly recommend backyard gardens, for reasons that have quite been overlooked and more so for the reason of surviving the current climate change leading to food shortages.

Backyard gardening is a must-do. Consider these.

1. Source of fresh and organic food.

Who wouldn't chose fresh and organic food?. Home gardens are very manageable and usually, in cases of insects and disease control, organic means could easily be applied. It is very important when you are very sure and have total control over the quality of food produced. You cannot be so sure of what is out there. Take advantage of that.

2. Gardening is a very good physical and mental exercise.

The experts say, gardening activities like soil preparation, planting, removal of weeds, watering, etc. engage most of your body muscles and are very good exercises. Gardening engages your mind too. They say, gardening 45 minutes early mornings each day before any other work, prepares you physically and mentally like 30 minutes of aerobics.

3. Supplements family budgets.

In our region, many families' (usually large) expenditure on food is greatly reduced. These are families that actively grow home gardens and they are able to cut down expenditure on food to about 40%. Adding to this, they are sure of the quality of the produce. This has been a major incentive for many to plant home gardens in many households. Some families only need to buy cooking oil and spices and the rest comes from their gardens.

4. Year-round food availability from gardens.

Since gardens are relatively small in land size, irrigation is easier and so continuous food supply through the seasons. Try it.

5. Gardening makes good use of space and protects the soil.

Putting it this way; we use the soil space around the house to plant a garden that gives all the benefits stated above and the one below. Plus, when we cover the soil with beneficial cover crops, erosion is reduced and regular bush growth around the house is minimised. Hope we have made that point clearer.

6. Entertainment, fulfilment and creativity.

The one having the experience can well explain this point. It is a good feeling. Try it. Gardening is a source of entertainment and really brings out lots of creativity in you. The art of planting various crops in the soil, nurturing them and watching them grow by the day and finally so see them blossom into fruits, is such a good feeling. You would be proud to say at the dining table, "this food is from my garden". So fulfilled.

Things to Know About Starting a Backyard Garden From Scratch

Gardening can easily become a lifelong hobby with no limit to the knowledge you can develop. But there are some basic skills you will need right from the beginning as you create your first planting bed. Here are nine gardening aspects to help you get started.

1. Grass Removal

Establishing a new garden bed often means sacrificing a portion of the lawn. You can kill grass (or other ground cover) with chemicals, though this is often harmful for you and the environment. There also are several effective organic methods of removing grassand the roots that go along with it.

Sheet Mulching (Layering)

Known as sheet mulching or layering, this method involves putting down layers of some organic material, such as newspaper or unwaxed cardboard, to smother the grass.1 It can take several months, but it is typically an effective way to kill grass. It is also organic and not harmful to the environment, as both the grass and the newspaper or cardboard simply break down and can be mixed with the soil.

Start by defining your planting bed, and then lay a thick layer of cardboard or newspaper over the grass. Ensure that any seams overlap by at least 6 inches. If you're using newspaper, make sure the sheets have black ink only (no color), and layer them at least 10 sheets thick. Then, add a layer of compost 3 to 4 inches thick over the paper or cardboard to hold it down. Wood chips will also work.

In warm climates, the grass will break down in about 3 or 4 months; in cooler climates, it might take an entire growing season.1 Once completed, add a thick layer of compost over the top of the planting bed. Your bed is now ready for flowers and shrubs.

Solarization

Another natural method is solarization: killing grass and weeds by utilizing the heat of the sun to bake the soil to a high temperature.

Start by mowing the grass in the planting area as short as possible. Then, hose down the area to dampen it thoroughly. Next, cover the area with a clear plastic tarp that's been cut to the desired size of your new garden space. With a moderate amount of sun exposure, the ground beneath the plastic can heat to around 140 degrees Fahrenheit. This will scorch living grass, as well as weeds, seeds, and soil bacteria.

Within about four weeks, your grass should be dead and beginning to break down. You can then dig the dead grass into the soil, adding compost or other soil amendments if you wish, and plant your garden bed.

Manual Removal

Manually removing grass is a lot of work, but it is great exercise and entirely natural. It's also very effective.

Moisten the lawn area thoroughly a day or two before you plan to remove the grass. This will soften the turf and loosen the root system. Next, use a sharp spade to cut the lawn into 1-square-foot sections. Remove each section by sliding the spade beneath the segment and levering it up and out of the ground.

The unwanted grass can be placed in a compost bin or discarded with other yard waste. But be aware that unless your composting process delivers sufficient heat, some grass seeds will likely survive and might sprout new grass when you eventually use the compost in the garden.

2. Garden Soil

Healthy soil is the foundation that makes any garden a success, and most plants have an optimal soil type in which they thrive. Common issues with soil that can affect the health of your plants include:

• Nutritional problems: Plants derive all of their nutrients from the soil. Perform a soil test on your garden bed. If the results suggest a deficiency, you'll need to add the necessary amendments to remedy the problem.

• Incorrect soil pH: Many plants tolerate a fairly wide range of soil pH levels, from acidic to alkaline. But soil that is too acidic or too alkaline will have trouble growing certain plants. Your soil test will also give you information on your garden soil's pH.

• Incorrect soil type: The soil type refers to the texture and composition of the soil. For instance, some soil contains too much clay, causing drainage problems. And other soil is too sandy, draining water before plant roots can make use of it.

Furthermore, no matter how good your soil is, you can't go wrong adding compostto it when you first start a garden. Work the compost into the soil with a rototiller or by hand. Then, rake the ground level to prepare it for planting.

You do not need fancy compost bins to make compost. Once you have grasped the basic concept of layering organic materials and providing just the right amount of moisture and air, composting is quite easy. Tiny natural organisms will quickly turn organic waste into the most nutritious soil additive available.

3. Plant Types

As you select your first plants, there are several qualities you should understand about them. First, plants commonly used in landscaping generally fall into certain classes:

• Herbaceous annuals: These are plants that go through their entire lifecycle in one growing season. Many flowers fall into this category, including marigolds, impatiens, petunias, zinnias, and cornflowers. In addition, some plants that perform as perennials in warm climates can be used as annuals in cold climates.

• Herbaceous perennials (and biennials): These are plants that return every year, often dying back to the ground in the winter but regrowing from the roots the following spring. Some perennials are very long-lived, such as peony and daylily, while others are relatively short-lived, such as lupine, columbine, and delphinium. Moreover, plants categorized as biennials can be considered very short-lived perennials. They often spend their first year developing and then flower in their second year before dying. Foxglove, hollyhock, and sweet William are examples of biennials.

• Woody trees and shrubs: These are plants that do not have the soft herbaceous stems of annuals and perennials. Instead, they have woody stems and trunks. Rather than dying back and regrowing from ground level, these plants sprout their new growth from a main trunk or main branches. All common trees fall into this category, as well as many bushes and shrubs.

• Vegetables, fruits, and herbs: These are generally defined as any plant that offers edible seeds, fruit, stems, or roots. Most are annual plants, though there are some biennials (carrots) and perennials (asparagus, strawberries). Plus, some are woody shrubs and trees, such as blueberries, peaches, and apples.

Furthermore, plants are categorized according to their growing needs, starting with their appropriate USDA hardiness zones. The hardiness zone map divides the U.S. into 13 areas, and plants are assigned zone numbers based on the climate in which they thrive. The cold limit is especially important, as this denotes the point on the map where winter temperatures will start to kill a plant.

In addition to the climate, plants have specific light and water requirements for optimal growth. It's ideal to group plants with similar needs in a garden bed for easier care.

If there's a chance you might not remember the names of what you've planted, consider labeling your plants by writing their names on a small wooden stake placed near them. That way, you'll be able to look up their growing needs if necessary. Plus, some gardeners like to keep a journal that maps the plants and layout of their garden each season.

4. Plant Arrangement

In addition to understanding plant types, you'll also need to develop some skill at garden design. This is largely a matter of personal preference, but there are a few standard design aesthetic tips to consider when arranging your plants.

Size

Take into consideration the mature size of plants when you first populate your garden bed. In general, a garden bed should be organized so the low-lying plants are in the foreground or used as edging, the medium-size plants are occupying the middle section, and the tall plants are in the background. The rules shift a little with an island garden, where it can be viewed from all angles. In that case, the center of the bed gets the tallest plants, and the smallest plants are on the perimeter.

Form

Garden designers frequently speak of plant form as a guiding principle when arranging plants. This essentially means that you should consider the overall shape or outline of the plants when arranging them in your garden bed. In general, if you seek a formal look, try to use precise geometric plant shapes, such as squared-off hedges and neat edging plants. If you want a more informal look, irregular forms are appropriate.

Line

When garden designers use the term line, it often refers to the structures within the landscape or garden bed—the edges of the garden, for example. It also can refer to the directional impact of the plants. Plants can have general vertical lines (a columnar evergreen), or they can be spreading and horizontal (a creeping juniper). Straight lines and hard angles give a formal look, while curved lines offer a casual feeling.

Texture

The term plant texture refers to the fineness or coarseness, roughness or smoothness, heaviness or lightness of a particular plant. The texture comes from a plant's flowers, stems, bark, and especially its leaves. To create variety and visual interest, make sure to use plants with different textures in the garden bed.

5. Color Schemes

In addition to size, form, line, and texture, one of the most important considerations when choosing plants is their color—both of the foliage and the flowers.2 Landscape designers put considerable effort into creating garden color schemes, but home gardeners should not feel too much pressure to follow technical design principles. Simply pay attention to the colors you're working with, so you like the ultimate look of your garden.

Warm and Cool Colors

An easy place to start is by understanding warm and cool colors, which have different attributes:

• Warm colors include shades of yellow, red, and orange. They are said to excite viewers.

• Cool colors include blue, purple, and green. They are said to calm and relax viewers.

This color theory can be used to create a garden suitable for a specific purpose. For example, a meditation garden can be planted with relaxing cool colors, while you might want to plant flowers with warm colors around a deck intended for parties and entertainment.

Unity and Contrast

Designing a garden with colors all within the cool family or the warm family is a means of creating unity. On the other hand, you might want to contrast warm and cool colors. Using complementary colors—color pairs found opposite one another on the color wheel—can add visual interest. For example, purple and yellow are frequently used in a complementary, contrasting color scheme.

6. Planting and Transplanting

Proper planting technique—whether it be from seeds or potted nursery plants—is critical for good results when gardening. Seed packets will have detailed information on how to plant what's inside.The information that comes with nursery plants is more sparse. In general, potted specimens need a planting hole roughly the size of their root ball, along with regular watering as the roots take hold.

In addition, soil temperature is critical when planting. Planting too early in the season when the soil is cool might result in a sickly plant all season long. But the same plant will flourish when started weeks later in a warm ground.

Furthermore, it's common for gardeners to move some plants around. Maybe they want the space for something else, or they decide they don't like the design. Whatever the reason, many plants can be successfully transplanted. Follow the transplanting advice for your specific plant, and work carefully and patiently for best results.

7. Weeds

Weeds are a gardener's enemy, so it's important to arm yourself with some facts about them. You first should know exactly which weedsyou are dealing with.

This knowledge will continue to come in handy long after you start a garden. Weeds will pop up again and again in spite of your best efforts to prevent them. There are many sources of information to help you identify weeds. Gardening books and university extension service websites often have photos of common weeds and offer tips on controlling them.

Furthermore, experienced gardeners quickly learn not everything that seems to be a weed really is one. Many plants, especially annual flowers, freely self-seed in the garden. So if you automatically remove every plant you don't recognize, you might be sacrificing flowers you would enjoy. For instance, snapdragons, petunias, aquilegia (columbine), foxglove (digitalis), and marigolds are some flowers that self-seed. But at the same time, this self-seeding tendency can become a nuisance by putting plants where you don't want them, effectively turning a flower into a weed.

8. Landscape Fabric

Landscape fabric is a synthetic textile that goes over a planting area to prevent weeds from sprouting up. It works by blocking the sunlight that is necessary for weed seeds to germinate. Holes can be cut in the fabric to insert garden plants, and then the fabric can be covered with mulch to hide it. Because the fabric is porous, water drains straight through to the ground. To prevent grass and other plants from invading your new bed, lay down some edging, as well.

A good place to use landscape fabric is in a shrub bed. When planting a group of landscape shrubs, simply lay down some fabric and cut holes to plant your shrubs. The bed should stay fairly weed-free for years.

Densely planted garden beds aren't as appropriate for landscape fabric. For example, if you are opening up ground for a cottage garden, the plants are usually packed tightly together. It can be difficult to cut many holes in a sheet of landscape fabric for this kind of garden bed.

9. Pests

All gardeners face pests at some point. In some instances, you can take preventive measures. For example, if you know your region has deer, select deer-resistant plants. Or if you've seen rabbits hopping around in your yard, surround your garden beds with rabbit-proof fences. There also are plants that deter certain insects.

But in some cases, you will have to take offensive measures. There are natural and synthetic chemical ways to combat pests, and each method has its pros and cons. Some natural methods might take longer to work while chemical methods can be harsh on the environment.

Furthermore, it's important to realize that good gardens are naturally diverse, and there are acceptable numbers of pests that can be tolerated. Attempting to entirely eradicate one pest sometimes can open the door to devastation by another pest. Your goal should be to maintain balance for a healthy garden.

CONCLUSION

Whatever your reason for setting up a garden in your backyard, it is strongly encouraged that you have the right tools and supplies on hand for maintaining your plants. You will definitely want to have gardening gloves (preferably with padded fingers/palms) that protect the hands, a sturdy kneeling pad that will protect your joints during those long weeding sessions, a strong steel topped shovel for removing stubborn weeds and shifting through tightly packed earth, and you want to have a wheelbarrow on hand to make the transporting of supplies, water jugs, soil and whatnot smoother.

How to Start a Backyard Garden

1. Be smart before you plant seeds to die.

Take note of your environment before you dive elbow-deep in soil. In her book, Churchill profiles Lauri Kranz, a garden decorator who's worked with clients like Adam Scott and Maya Rudolph. In initial consultations, Kranz will analyze the prospective site and determine what plants will thrive in that situation. "Not every plant works in every place," Kranz says in the book. "The plant will let us know where it wants to be, where it will thrive. All we need to do is pay attention."

Churchill recommends starting small, with one or two plants, to see how you feel with the initial responsibility. The gardening doesn't necessarily need to start in the backyard. "Use what you have around you, whatever that is — a windowsill, indoor planter or herb garden, a fire escape, a backyard or a farm," Churchill says. Test the waters with your first plant and get a feel for the new hobby.

To decide what kind of plants you should start growing, be conscious of where you live. Research what plants are native to where you are, and those varietals will thrive in your backyard. They'll also be more forgiving if you forget that you've recently become a plant parent.

2. Be patient.

You're taking care of a living, breathing thing. Don't expect to wake up one morning and suddenly find a jungle in your backyard.

"It can be rewarding to see little shoots from zucchini or squash pop up and grow so quickly, but it can just as often take years from a tree to come into its own, a lilac to really unveil its blossoms or young plantings to take form," Churchill says. Every bit of attention that goes towards the garden will be tenfold as rewarding.

While the path to a lush garden is long and slow, the final product will be the result of a combination of your love and care and nature's good graces. Once you've found your groove, you'll want to diversify the types of plants you grow to ensure that there's always something blooming throughout the year.

3. Get the right gear.

Gardening requires a new set of tools. To start, Churchill recommends seeds from Row 7. Row 7, co-founded by Dan Barber of the Michelin-starred Blue Hill restaurant, sells seeds that were specially bred to grow produce with enhanced flavor, more so than the stuff you'll find in supermarkets. The hori hori knife is an essential gardening tool thanks to a serrated edge, pointed end and curved design. Churchill is partial to the Carbon Steel Hori Hori knife from Hida Tools), and they're the choice tool for weeding, digging and cutting.

Churchill's grail is a pair of Niwaki S-Type Clippers for cutting and pruning her plants. Clippers are important for maintaining plants' shape and for fielding any unruly growth. To keep her tools in order, Churchill boasts about the Canvas Carry-All Garden Stool from Terrain. Gardening can be strenuous, particularly on the knees, and this two-in-one carry-all doubles as a foldaway stool.

4. Reap the benefits of your work.

Churchill recalls the first time she planted a shiso seed and watched it flourish in a matter of months. While the world continues to reel from the effects of the coronavirus pandemic, nurturing a garden and watching it grow into something remarkable reminds us that there is still beauty in this world.

"I think gardening is a direct, tangible way to appreciate and care for the natural world," Churchill says. "It teaches you to view the world around you differently, with more respect, and to treat it more tenderly."

Growing food can often save you money. There are, of course, initial startup costs. Depending on the space you have, you may need to buy pots, compost, soil, seeds, materials to make raised beds, etc. However, when you start to reap the rewards of your work, it can significantly cut down on grocery store costs.

www.ingramcontent.com/pod-product-compliance
Lightning Source LLC
Chambersburg PA
CBHW020516160726
47991CB00007B/2983